★★★ EDITED AND WITH A FOREWORD BY MICHAEL ALLEN ★★★★

AMERICA'S FEDERAL HOLIDAYS
★★★★★★★★ THE TRUE STORY ★★★★★★★★★

JOHN DE GREE

Celebrating America's Federal Holidays
by John De Gree
Published by The Classical Historian,
copyright© 2014 by The Classical Historian.
All Rights Reserved.
Printed in The United States of America.
No part of this book my be used or reproduced in any manner whatsoever without written permission except in the case of a brief quotation embodied in critical articles and reviews.
Design: Pearpod

More info:
Classical Historian
1019 Domador
San Clemente, CA 92673
714.623.6104
John@ClassicalHistorian.Com

TABLE OF CONTENTS

FOREWORD	7
INTRODUCTION	8
NEW YEAR'S DAY	10
MARTIN LUTHER KING JR'S BIRTHDAY	14
INAUGURATION DAY	18
GEORGE WASHINGTON'S BIRTHDAY	22
MEMORIAL DAY	26
INDEPENDENCE DAY	30
LABOR DAY	34
COLUMBUS DAY	38
VETERAN'S DAY	44
THANKSGIVING DAY	48
CHRISTMAS DAY	54

FOREWORD BY MICHAEL ALLEN

I am very happy that John De Gree's *America's Federal Holidays* is now in print. There is no other book quite like it, and it will prove extremely valuable to classroom teachers in America's public, private, charter, and home schools.

How many of today's elementary, secondary, and college students really understand the origins and meaning of the days they get to "take off" during the school year or their summer vacations? Unfortunately, students (and sometimes their parents and teachers!) become absorbed in the joy of the impending long weekend and forget "the reason for the season," as it were. How many of us could, off the tops of our heads, thoroughly and accurately state the historic origins of Memorial Day? New Year's Day? And while the roots of celebrating the Fourth of July and Christmas may seem obvious, in fact there is much more to the stories of these "days off" than we know. It is thus very important to make *America's Federal Holidays* part of the effort to train good citizens in our schools.

John De Gree is a seasoned classroom teacher with many years' experience in both public and private schools. His website and curriculum, *The Classical Historian,* is subscribed to by thousands of public, private, homeschool, and charter school parents and teachers. And John De Gree and his wife Zdenka are parents and teachers to their own seven children. This experience is obvious in each of the pages that follow. John's lessons on Labor Day, Columbus Day, Veterans Day, Thanksgiving, Dr. Martin Luther King's Birthday, George Washington's Birthday, and all other official federal holidays are brimming with information that will make for good classroom learning. *America's Federal Holidays* will help teachers create lesson plans to use immediately prior to the respective holiday vacations.

On occasion, Americans appear more concerned with taking a well-earned vacation than pondering the reasons for the blessed event. "Blessed" is an apt term here, because all holidays stem historically from religious "days of rest" and, of course, the Sabbath. Indeed, one of the remarkable things we learn from *America's Federal Holidays* is that religion and religious motives form the basis for most of our federally recognized holidays.

So, the next time you get to take a three-day weekend, enjoy it! But before you do, read through John De Gree's America's *Federal Holidays* to understand why.

Michael Allen

PROFESSOR OF HISTORY, UNIVERSITY OF WASHINGTON, TACOMA

CO-AUTHOR, *A PATRIOT'S HISTORY OF THE UNITED STATES* AND *A PATRIOT'S HISTORY READER*

#1 BEST SELLING NEW YORK TIMES AUTHOR

INTRODUCTION

Americans designate eleven days of the year as federal holidays. Over the past centuries, various United States Congresses and Presidents have set aside these days to honor and to teach the meaning of our country's most important people and events. For a republic to thrive, it is essential that its citizens take an active part in understanding and appreciating its heroes and most important events. Because citizens in a republic carry the duty to vote for able leaders and decide the direction of our country, knowledge of what make the United States unique and strong is essential.

Americans have forgotten the meaning behind its federal holidays. In efforts to revise our country's history and to increase our leisure time, our federal holidays have lost their power. We don't appreciate the peaceful passing of power from one party to another that takes place on Inauguration Day. We don't recall who inspired Dr. Martin Luther King, Jr. We overlook the courage and perseverance of George Washington, the Father of Our Country. Independence Day has become a day of fireworks and feasts, instead of a remembrance of liberty and sacrifices. Memorial Day and Labor Day have become a way to mark the beginning and ending of summer. Christopher Columbus has moved from a place of honor, to dislike, to ignorance in the minds of most. Many schoolchildren falsely believe the first Thanksgiving was held so the Pilgrims could thank the Indians. And Christmas, an official federal holiday, is a word that is not even uttered in public places for fear of offending someone.

America's Federal Holidays, The True Story™ promotes the heroic people and events that are the reason for America's federal holidays. This book will encourage Americans to appreciate the shared history of our people, understand the meaning behind each day, and strengthen our citizens and our republic. Knowledge and understanding of our history will help students realize the uniqueness of what it means to be an American, and will inspire students to be their best.

Honoring Excellence and Virtues Provides Examples for Youth

The American Founding Fathers taught that for a republic to thrive, patriotism would be necessary. In order for citizens to make informed judgments, be inspired to defend their country, and be productive citizens, they should know the decisions earlier Americans made that helped form our country. Americans should learn what inspired individuals to accomplish challenging tasks. In learning about the great accomplishments of those who came before us, we are inspired to achieve, as well. A country with no heroes has no future.

Federal holidays teach our youth about what is important to our country. Memorial Day is set aside to give honor to those fallen in battle protecting our liberty. Veteran's Day shows respect to veterans for sacrificing their time to serve our country. Young people should honor those who labor and reflect what job or occupation they might have in the future on Labor Day. Columbus Day gives honor to a person who brought Western civilization to North and South America. Learning how the Pilgrims survived in a state of thanksgiving to God teaches Americans how to be grateful during challenging times. Learning about a person born of humble origin who later sacrifices his life for others on Christmas will help teach youth what is true love.

People are Not Without Flaws

It has become common to claim that many of America's political heroes were actually men with serious flaws, and, the argument goes, we shouldn't honor them. When we honor George Washington, or Dr. Martin Luther King, Jr., or Christopher Columbus as great men who accomplished much for Western civilization, we are not claiming that these individuals were perfect. We are making the argument that without these individuals the United States may have lost the American Revolution, continued to practice segregation, or might have never been formed. These men are heroes for the country, but they are not examples of perfect men.

Uniform Monday Holiday Act

In 1968, an act of Congress changed the date Americans celebrate four holidays. This act declared that from 1971, Washington's Birthday (originally February 22), Memorial Day (May 30), Columbus Day (October 12), and Veterans Day (November 11) would all be celebrated on Mondays. The main reason for this was to enable federal workers and other Americans to have longer weekends. Later, Dr. Martin Luther King, Jr. Day was added on a Monday as well. The primary result of this act is that many Americans don't care about the people and events that are the reasons behind the federal holidays. They are just happy to have a three day weekend. Realizing this, in 1975, Congress placed Veterans Day back on November 11th to keep the practice of honoring veterans as the main reason for the holiday, however, it left all of the other "Monday Holidays" intact.

The Lessons

Lessons should be read out loud to students in classrooms and to whole families at home. Each lesson has a short essay that describes the most important parts of the holiday. Some lessons include primary source documents. These are followed by 10 text-dependent questions. These questions are designed for ages 8 and older, although there will be some younger children able to answer the questions, and, a few of the questions may be too challenging for some 8 year olds. After the 10 questions, there are a few questions marked "Research and Analysis." For this, the teacher may assign one or all of the activities for the student to do on his own. These activities are more challenging than the 10 text-dependent questions, and are appropriate for ages 12 and older.

★★★★ CHAPTER ONE ★★★★
NEW YEAR'S DAY

January 1st

New Year's Day in the United States of America has been celebrated for over two hundred years, but its history goes back thousands of years. In 2000 B.C., Mesopotamians celebrated the vernal equinox as the beginning of a new year. This practice continued through the Middle Ages, with many countries of the world celebrating the New Year on March 20th. However, in 1752, the British and their colonists in America adopted the Gregorian calendar, and from this time on, Americans have celebrated New Year's Day on January 1st.

What is the Vernal Equinox?

Vernal means "Spring", and equinox means "equal night". On the vernal equinox, March 20th, the sun is located above the equator and day and night are about equal length. For those living in the Northern Hemisphere, March 20th marks the beginning of Spring. After this day, there is an increasing amount of sunlight every day until the beginning of Summer, June 21. For ancient people, celebrating the vernal equinox as the New Year was very logical. People were moving away from darkness into the light. Agrarian people rely on the power of the sun in growing crops. For the ancients, the vernal equinox was a time to celebrate birth, sunlight, and fertility. Romans would exchange gifts and make promises they would try to fulfill in the new year.

Why Do We Celebrate New Year's Day on January 1st and not March 20th?

The United States of America and most Western countries trace much of their cultural heritage to the Roman Republic and to Judeo-Christian beliefs and practices. Before Julius Caesar, Romans celebrated March 1st as the New Year because March is the first month in the Roman calendar. Romans had a festival to honor their god, Mars (God of War). In 45 B.C., Julius Caesar reformed the Roman calendar and changed the celebration of the New Year to January 1st, in honor of Janus, the Roman god who January is named after. The god Janus was always shown with two faces, one looking to the past and one looking ahead. On this day, the Romans exchanged gifts and promised to be better with each other in the new year. Romans also celebrated this day by throwing parties with food, drink, and dancing.

The first Christian Roman Emperor, Constantine the Great (272 – 337), kept the Julian Calendar, but turned New Year's Day into a day of prayer and fasting. Christians were encouraged to use the day as a beginning to live better lives. From the seventh century on, January 1st was celebrated by Christians in the Roman Calendar as a day honoring The Solemnity of Mary, Mother of God. The Christian Church attempted to change the parties of the Roman times into a time of prayer and reflection.

★★★ CHAPTER ONE | NEW YEAR'S DAY ★★★

New Year's Parties Abolished

In 567 at the Council of Tours, Christians abolished the celebrations of January 1 because they considered them pagan. Instead, they celebrated the new year on December 25th, the day the Church chose to honor the birth of Jesus. However, there weren't mass celebrations of the new year, as knowledge of the exact date was not widespread.

Gregorian Calendar: January 1st Restored

In 1582, much of the Western world reformed the Julian Calendar because of its inaccuracies and adopted the Gregorian Calendar. Named after Pope Gregory III, the calendar restored January 1st as the New Year Day. Great Britain kept the Julian calendar until 1752, and it was at this time that the English colonists started celebrating January 1st as New Year's Day.

How do Americans Celebrate New Year's Day?

Americans celebrate New Year's Day in a variety of ways. On New Year's Eve, there are gatherings of friends and family the evening before to remember the year past and to look forward to the new year. There is revelry and merry making that takes place in private and public places. Some Americans make New Year's resolutions, with promises of working harder, losing weight, or enrolling in a class. Other Americans carry on the religious traditions of New Year's Day, as well. Anglicans and Lutherans mark the day as the Feast of the Circumcision of Christ, remembering the Christian belief that Christ was circumcised 8 days after birth. Roman Catholics celebrate this day remembering Mary as the mother of Jesus.

QUESTIONS:

1. When did Mesopotamians celebrate the new year?

2. What does the Vernal Equinox mean for those living in the Northern Hemisphere?

3. Who changed the celebration of the new year to January 1st in 45 B.C.?

4. Why was the date of the new year changed?

5. How did the Romans celebrate the new year?

6. How did Constantine the Great change the celebrating of the new year?

7. From the seventh century on, who did Christians honor on New Year's Day?

8. Throughout the first eight centuries, why did most people in the world not celebrate the new year?

9. When was the Gregorian Calendar adopted by most of the Western world?

10. How do people of various Christian faiths celebrate the new year religiously?

RESEARCH OR ANALYSIS:

Research the history of New Year's Day and find two ways people of the past celebrated the new year. Write these down and share them with your family or with classmates.

★★★★ CHAPTER TWO ★★★★
BIRTHDAY OF MARTIN LUTHER KING, JR.

Third Monday of January

On the third Monday of January, Americans celebrate the birthday of Dr. Martin Luther King, Jr, perhaps the most important leader of the Civil Rights Movement. King was born on January 15, 1929, in Atlanta, Georgia, in an American society that had strict laws and customs that were based on the color of your skin. This legal policy called segregation separated whites from non-whites in nearly all public places and limited the ability of black Americans to vote and completely enjoy the benefits that come with living in a free country. Raised in a strong Christian environment, Martin Luther King, Jr. believed that the best way to change the United States and end segregation was to win over the hearts of fellow Americans by following the teachings of Jesus Christ to "love your enemy" and by following the example of non-violent leaders such as the Indian Mahatma Ghandi. In large part due to Dr. King's words and example, Americans ended segregation in the 1960s and today enjoy perhaps one of the freest societies of the world, where people are judged "by the content of their character" and actions more than on their physical appearances. Tragically, on April 4, 1968, Dr. Martin Luther King, Jr. was assassinated by confirmed racist James Earl Ray.

History of Segregation

Racial segregation became a way of life in most southern states during the decades after Reconstruction ended in 1877. During Reconstruction, the U.S. attempted to "reconstruct" the Confederacy that had just lost the Civil War. Michael Allen and Larry Schweikart write in A *Patriot's History of the United States that in Reconstruction* (1867-1877), the U.S. attempted to readmit members of the Confederacy, rebuild the South, and help the freed men and women to live and work in a hostile environment. When Reconstruction ended, the northern soldiers went home, and the southern whites began to enact laws that separated whites from non-whites. In practice, segregation greatly limited black Americans' ability to work, kept black Americans from voting, and created a permanent underclass of blacks who did not enjoy the protection of the U.S. law. Economic and social mobility was nearly impossible for black Americans, and in many southern states, they were in constant physical danger. They were terrorized, brutalized, and murdered in astonishing numbers. The Supreme Court, in Plessy v Ferguson (1896) legalized racial segregation. Segregation was the legal policy of separating the races, and insured that black Americans would always constitute a permanent underclass.

Childhood

Martin grew up in a strong, religious family. Originally named Michael like his father, he changed his name after the famous founder of the Lutheran religion, Martin Luther. His grandfather founded the Ebenezer Baptist Church in Atlanta, and when he died, Martin's father became the pastor. Martin attended Booker T. Washington High School, where he skipped both the ninth and the eleventh grades and at age 15, entered Morehouse College in Atlanta in 1944. As a junior in college, he decided to follow in his father and grandfather's footsteps to become a pastor.

As a doctoral student of theology at Boston University, Martin met Coretta Scott, a singer and musician at the New England Conservatory. They married and eventually had four children. King received his Ph.D. in 1955 and became pastor at the Dexter Avenue Baptist Church of Montgomery, Alabama.

Love Your Enemy

In the 1950s, many in America realized that the policy of segregation was unjust and opposed to the basic ideals of the United States. Many black Americans had fought and sacrificed in World War II and were currently fighting and dying in Korea. It seemed horribly unfair, then, that at home, black Americans did not have equal rights with white Americans. Those who wanted to change segregation faced several choices. One was just to wait until things changed, somehow. Another option was to turn to violence and to force white America to change. Martin Luther King, Jr. chose a third option. A strong Christian and student of nonviolent methods, King believed that the most effective and just way to promote change in America was to love your neighbor and win over his heart. King's choice was not an easy one, and he bore the pain and suffering of his decision. However, his way of nonviolence and love most likely saved the lives of many, and brought about immense change in the United States.

The Civil Rights Movement

In 1955, a brave and simple act by Rosa Parks, a 42 year-old woman, advanced the Civil Rights Movement and the national leadership of Dr. Martin Luther King, Jr. In Montgomery buses, blacks had to sit in the back of the bus, and if there were no more white seats towards the front, blacks were supposed to stand and allow the whites to sit. Rosa Parks sat in the black section, but was ordered to stand by the bus driver because there were a few whites who had no seats. Parks refused to stand, was arrested, and fined. Black community leaders met and decided to fight the bus company, a privately owned business. They chose Dr. King, Jr. to lead a bus boycott and force the bus company to change its policy. After 382 days of avoiding bus travel, enduring harassment, violence, and intimidation, the blacks of Montgomery forced the company to desegregate its buses. The Civil Rights Movement had begun, and Dr. Martin Luther King, Jr. became the noted leader of peaceful, nonviolent resistance to the unjust system of segregation in America.

I Have a Dream

Dr. King, Jr. was involved in many more Civil Rights battles, was jailed, and was eventually murdered for his desire to see a color-free American society. A moving orator, King, Jr. is most recognized for his "I Have a Dream" speech given in Washington, D.C. in 1963. King spoke of his dream of an America where children would grow up in a country where they would be judged based on the content of their character and not the color of their skin. Segregation officially ended in the United States by the passage of various laws in the 1960s.

On April 4, 1968, Dr. King, Jr. was assassinated by white supremacist James Earl Ray. Ray fled the country, was found in London, convicted, and sentenced to 99 years in jail.

Four days after King's death Congressmen began an effort to have a federal holiday in honor of King, Jr. However, some Americans felt that he was just one person of many in the Civil Rights Movement. In 1983, President Ronald Reagan signed into law holiday legislation, making the third Monday in January the day to honor Dr. King, Jr. Even after the federal holiday was declared, several southern states included celebrations for various Confederate generals on that day, and some states protested.

QUESTIONS:

1. When was Dr. King, Jr. born?

2. What was his original name?

3. Why did he change his name?

4. What was his wife's name and how many children did they have?

5. What grades did Martin skip in high school?

6. What was Dr. King, Jr.'s occupation?

7. Explain why religion was important to Dr. King, Jr.

8. What was segregation?

9. How did the Civil Rights Movement begin?

10. Who were Dr. King's role models and how did these role models affect Dr. King, Jr.?

RESEARCH OR ANALYSIS:

1. Dr. King, Jr. believed that for a non-violent protest to work, protesters had to show the rest of the country how the actions of some were horrible. For example, Dr. King, Jr. planned marches in areas where there was strong hatred of desegregationists, perhaps knowing that his demonstrators would possibly be injured. In these demonstrations, policemen and firemen would spray demonstrators with strong fire hoses, or they would unleash attack dogs. Some have said that Dr. King's methods were not good, because of this, and that it was King who was causing the violence. What do you think? In your answer, explain why you think the way you do.

2. Dr. King, Jr. spoke of a color-free America, where people would be judged on the quality of their character, and not the color of their skin. To what extent do you think this is true today? What evidence do you have to support your answer?

3. Racial quotas means when an institution, such as a university, decides that it wants to admit a certain percentage of students because of the color of their skin, even if there are more qualified applicants. Do you think Dr. King, Jr. would support or oppose this? Why do you think this?

★★★★ CHAPTER THREE ★★★★
INAUGURATION DAY

January 20th or 21st

Inauguration Day is the federal holiday set aside as the beginning of the new presidential term. The main and only requirement of the day is for the president to take the oath of office, though there are a number of other activities that occur. Originally, Inauguration Day was on March 4th, the day the U.S. Constitution took effect. Since the Twentieth Amendment in 1933, Inauguration Day has been January 20th or 21st, if the 20th falls on a Sunday.

Article Two, Section One, Clause Eight of the Constitution includes the wording of the oath of office:

I do solemnly swear (or affirm) that I will faithfully execute the Office of President of the United States, and will to the best of my Ability, preserve, protect and defend the Constitution of the United States.

The President may substitute the word "affirm" for "swear." It is believed the Framers of the Constitution included this option because of the Quaker literal interpretation of a passage in the New Testament to not use swear words.

When the American experiment began, few had faith in the world of its success. Most believed that a republic could not survive. People thought that citizens were not capable of voting for leaders. When Thomas Jefferson won the presidency and political power shifted from the Federalist Party to the Democratic-Republican Party, it was a major event not for what happened, but for what did not occur. There was no fighting in the streets. No war broke out. Everywhere was peace. In many countries of the world, when one faction takes power from another, a war follows. Inauguration Day in America is a testament to the strength and durability of a republic.

Certain elements of the inaugural ceremony are steeped in tradition but are not a requirement for taking the oath of office. George Washington took the oath of office with his left hand on a Bible, and his right hand raised. After saying the oath, he kissed the Bible. Many presidents after followed this example. John Quincy Adams took the oath with his hand on a book of law. When President Obama took the oath of office in 2013, he uttered the words, "So help me God" at the end. It is believed that President Washington started this tradition, though historians are not sure about it.

After taking the oath of office, the U.S. President gives his speech, the Inaugural Address. The form and words have changed greatly over time. Below are excerpts of a few addresses:

Excerpt from President Washington's First Inaugural Address, April 30, 1789:

Having thus imparted to you my sentiments as they have been awakened by the occasion which brings us together, I shall take my present leave; but not without resorting once more to the benign Parent of the Human Race in humble supplication that, since He has been pleased to favor the American people with opportunities for deliberating in perfect tranquility, and dispositions for deciding with unparalleled unanimity on a form of government for the security of their union and the advancement of their happiness, so His divine blessing may be equally 'conspicuous' in the enlarged views, the temperate consultations, and the wise measures on which the success of this Government must depend.

CHAPTER THREE | INAUGURATION DAY

Excerpt from President Lincoln's Second Inaugural Address, March 4, 1865:

With malice toward none, with charity for all, with firmness in the right as God gives us to see the right, let us strive on to finish the work we are in, to bind up the nation's wounds, to care for him who shall have borne the battle and for his widow and his orphan, to do all which may achieve and cherish a just and lasting peace among ourselves and with all nations.

Excerpt from President Franklin Roosevelt's Third Inaugural Address, January 20, 1941:

In the face of great perils never before encountered, our strong purpose is to protect and to perpetuate the integrity of democracy.

For this we muster the spirit of America, and the faith of America.

We do not retreat. We are not content to stand still. As Americans, we go forward, in the service of our country, by the will of God.

Excerpt from President John Kennedy's Inaugural Address, January 20, 1961

In the long history of the world, only a few generations have been granted the role of defending freedom in its hour of maximum danger. I do not shrink from this responsibility—I welcome it. I do not believe that any of us would exchange places with any other people or any other generation. The energy, the faith, the devotion which we bring to this endeavor will light our country and all who serve it—and the glow from that fire can truly light the world.

Excerpt from President Ronald Reagan's Inaugural Address, January 20, 1981

If we look to the answer as to why, for so many years, we achieved so much, prospered as no other people on Earth, it was because here, in this land, we unleashed the energy and individual genius of man to a greater extent than has ever been done before. Freedom and the dignity of the individual have been more available and assured here than in any other place on Earth. The price for this freedom at times has been high, but we have never been unwilling to pay that price.

QUESTIONS:

1. What is inauguration day?

2. When does it take place?

3. What did Washington put his left hand on when he took the oath of office?

4. What four words did President Obama utter after he took the oath of office?

5. What is the Inaugural Address?

6. Who is Washington referring to in his Inaugural Address when he states "since He has been pleased to favor the American people with opportunities for deliberating in perfect tranquility?"

7. Paraphrase the following section from Lincoln's speech: "With malice toward none, with charity for all, with firmness in the right as God gives us to see the right,"

8. Paraphrase the following from Roosevelt's speech: "As Americans, we go forward, in the service of our country, by the will of God."

9. John F. Kennedy spoke about the challenging of fighting communism in the following quote, "In the long history of the world, only a few generations have been granted the role of defending freedom in its hour of maximum danger. I do not shrink from this responsibility—I welcome it." Based on this quote, what was his intention in this challenge?

10. According to Ronald Reagan, why has America prospered?

RESEARCH OR ANALYSIS:

1. Paraphrase one or all excerpts of the Inaugural Addresses in this lesson.

2. Research and write what the historical context was of one or more of the Inaugural Addresses in this lesson. (What was happening in the U.S. and in the world at the time the Presidents gave these speeches?)

3. Read three inaugural addresses and choose one that you find most stirring. Share this speech with your family or class.

CHAPTER FOUR
WASHINGTON'S BIRTHDAY

February 18th

George Washington (1732-1799)

I. Early Life

George Washington is called The Father of our Country. This title is significant. Without a father, there can be no family. Many historians say that without George Washington, there could be no United States of America.

George Washington grew up on his family's tobacco plantation. His family owned slaves and was moderately wealthy. As a little boy, George was known for swimming in the nearby river, playing outside, riding horses, and taking his studies seriously. We think George studied under Reverend James Marye, rector of St. George's Parish, though he never attended college.

In the 1700s, death was much more common than it is today due to poorer medical knowledge and practice. George's father Augustine's first wife died. His father remarried to Mary and they had six children. George was Augustine and Mary's first baby, and he was born on February 22, 1732 in Virginia. Augustine and Mary lost three children, two dying in infancy, and one at the age of 12. When George was 11, his father died.

As a young man, Washington attended church at St. George's Parish in Fredericksburg. Along with his religious training, he learned how to behave in society by writing and reflecting on a book entitled Rules of Civility & Decent Behaviour In Company and Conversation. The book survives today.

George Washington took dancing lessons, went to the theater, and was a superb horseman. He was tall, especially for the 1700s, at 6 feet, 2 inches. George paid close attention to behaving like a gentleman, and is known for having a commanding presence.

II. Military Life

In the 1700s, France, Spain, and England all wanted to control North America. Washington joined the Virginia militia and rose to the rank of major. In the French and Indian War (1756-1763), the English fought the French and Indians for control of the Ohio Valley. In The Battle of Monongahela, the British General Braddock was killed, and every other officer was shot, except Washington. Washington was forced to take over and skillfully lead the British and Virginian forces in retreat. Riding on his horse, back and forth among his soldiers in plain sight of the enemy, his actions saved perhaps hundreds of soldiers. On that day, the Indians shot and killed two of Washington's horses while he was riding them, but they couldn't kill Washington.

After the battle, his coat had bullet holes on both the front and the back. It is said that as President, an Indian warrior visited him and said these words, "White Father. I was there at the Battle of Monongahela. We were victorious that day and had shot all of the officers off of their horses but you. I told my men to aim at you, but after many efforts to kill you, we realized that The Great Spirit was protecting you, and we stopped firing on you."

General Washington achieved his greatest military success during the American Revolution (1775-1783). Named Commander of the Continental Army, Washington raised an army from farmers and other volunteers. He

★★★★ CHAPTER FOUR | WASHINGTON'S BIRTHDAY ★★★★

trained the Americans into a professional fighting force, and defeated the greatest empire in the world. It is difficult to overstate his accomplishments in the American Revolution. In the battles he lost, such as The Battle of Long Island in the summer of 1776, he craftily led his army out of a terrible trap so they could fight another day. Battles he won, such as the Battle of Trenton and the Battle of Princeton, gave the American army courage that they could win the war. In the last battle of the war, the Battle of Yorktown, he tricked one of the world's best generals, General Cornwallis, and captured, killed, or wounded Cornwallis' entire army.

III. Presidency

Washington served as President from 1789-1797. He strengthened the national government and set a precedent that Presidents would not become kings. During his service, he worked hard to make Americans see themselves as Americans first, and not as citizens of the various states or as people who were French-American or English-American. When citizens in Pennsylvania violently protested a tax on whiskey, Washington ordered 13,000 U.S. soldiers to march and put down the revolt.

When Washington was asked to serve a third term, he refused and went back to being a farmer in Virginia. Because of his example of humility, all subsequent presidents for over 130 years only served two terms. Within a few years of retiring from public life, Washington became sick and died at his home, Mount Vernon, in 1799

IV. Federal Holiday

In 1880, an act of Congress declared George Washington's birthday as a federal holiday. It is the first national holiday honoring an American citizen. Washington's birthday is celebrated today on the third Monday of February.

QUESTIONS:

1. Which American has the title 'Father of our Country' and why?

2. What did Washington do as a young boy?

3. List the people who died in George Washington's family before he turned 12 years old:

4. Which war did Washington fight in as an officer in the British Army?

5. What was Washington's position in the Continental Army during The American Revolution?

6. What was one important precedent Washington set as President of the U.S.A?

7. In which century did Washington live in?

8. How did Washington respond to the tax revolt in Pennsylvania?

9. How did Washington distinguish himself at the Battle of Long Island?

10. At which battle did Washington receive bullet holes in the front and back of his coat?

RESEARCH OR ANALYSIS:

1. After reading, research George Washington's Rules of Civility. What is your opinion of these rules?

2. Write a short paragraph answering this question, "What did George Washington do that encouraged Americans to call him the "Father of the Country?"

CHAPTER FIVE
MEMORIAL DAY

The Last Monday of May

Memorial Day is a federal holiday set aside to honor all American soldiers who have fallen in battle. In 1967, Congress and the President Lyndon Johnson set aside May 30th as Memorial Day, but the history of this day goes back at least to the end of the American Civil War. Americans remember our fallen soldiers by attending church services and praying for military families, visiting war museums, and remembering loved ones who died fighting by placing flowers on graves of deceased American warriors.

Honoring the Civil War Dead

More Americans died in the American Civil War than in all other American wars combined. An estimated 625,000 American soldiers died, including about 30% of all Southern white males and 10 percent of Northern males ages 20-45. Nearly every American knew someone who died. The sheer numbers of death and casualties in America had a great impact on the living, and immediately, Americans spontaneously acted to honor those who gave their lives.

In both the South and North, Americans strove to honor those who died fighting for their country. The United States government established national cemeteries for the Union dead. But what started the practice of Memorial Day was not an official governmental act, but thousands of individual acts of tenderness and care that survivors showed to the graves of fallen soldiers of the Civil War. Communities held "Decoration Days," where people walked to the cemetery to decorate the gravestones of fallen soldiers.

One of the first known observances of a mass Decoration Day was in Charleston, South Carolina, on May 1, 1865. 257 Union prisoners had died during the war in a Charleston war prison and had been buried there. Freed slaves, along with missionaries and others, organized a celebration in May. Some in the North have called this the "First Decoration Day." On this day, more than 10,000 people, including 3,000 newly freed children, participated.

Official Holiday

Throughout the late 1800s and early 1900s, the American Army, the U.S. government, and individual states celebrated Decoration Day, usually on May 30th, a date chosen because no great battle fell on this day. In 1967, Memorial Day became an official holiday, originally set to May 30th. In 1968, Congress passed a law which moved four holidays to the closest Monday to create convenient three-day weekends. Unfortunately, this move has caused most Americans to view holidays such as Memorial Day as an opportunity for mere recreation, instead of trying to honor our fallen soldiers.

Normandy

On June 6, 1984, on the fortieth anniversary of D-Day, President Ronald Reagan gave a speech in front of the U.S. Ranger Monument at Normandy, commemorating the Rangers' charge up Pointe du Hoc.

"Forty summers have passed since the battle that you fought here. You were young the day you took these cliffs; some of you were hardly more than boys, with the deepest joys of life before you. Yet, you risked everything here. Why? Why did you do it? What impelled you to put aside the instinct for self-preservation and risk your lives to take these cliffs? What inspired all the men of the armies that met here? We look at you, and somehow we know the answer. It was faith and belief; it was loyalty and love.

The men of Normandy had faith that what they were doing was right, faith that they fought for all humanity, faith that a just God would grant them mercy on this beachhead or on the next. It was the deep knowledge – and pray God we have not lost it – that there is a profound, moral difference between the use of force for liberation and the use of force for conquest. You were here to liberate, not to conquer, and so you and those others did not doubt your cause. And you were right not to doubt.

You all knew that some things are worth dying for. One's country is worth dying for, and democracy is worth dying for, because it's the most deeply honorable form of government ever devised by man. All of you loved liberty."

★★★ CHAPTER FIVE | MEMORIAL DAY ★★★★

Below are listed all American military deaths that occurred in the various wars fought by the United States of America.

Conflict	Deaths	Span
American Revolution	25,000	1775-1783
Northwest Indian War	1,056	1785-1795
French Quasi-War	514	1798-1800
War of 1812	20,000	1812-1815
1st Seminole War	36	1817-1818
Black Hawk War	305	1832
2nd Seminole War	1,535	1835-1842
Mexican-American War	13,283	1846-1848
3rd Seminole War	26	1855-1858
Civil War	625,000	1861-1865
Great Plains Indian Wars	919	1865-1898
Great Sioux War	314	1875-1877
Spanish-America War	2,446	1898
Philippine-American War	4,196	1898-1913
Chinese Boxer Rebellion	131	1900-1901
Mexican Revolution	35	1914-1919
Haiti Occupation	148	1915-1934
World War 1	116,516	1917-1918
North Russia Campaign	424	1918-1920
American Exped. Force Siberia	328	1918-1920
Nicaragua Occupation	48	1927-1933
World War 2	405,399	1941-1945
Korean War	36,516	1950-1953
Vietnam War	58,209	1955-1975
El Salvador Civil War	37	1980-1992
Beirut	266	1982-1984
Grenada	19	1983
Panama	40	1989
Persian Gulf War	258	1990-1991
Operation Provide Comfort	19	1991-1996
Somalia Intervention	43	1992-1995
Bosnia	12	1995-2004
NATO Air Campaign Yugoslavia	20	1999
The War on Terror		
a. Afghanistan (ongoing)	2,229	2001-
b. Iraq	4,488	2003-2011

wikipedia.org/wiki/United_States_military_casualties_of_war
taken on Nov 18, 2013

QUESTIONS:

1. Order the five most dangerous American wars, in terms of American deaths.

2. After which war did Americans begin to celebrate Decoration Day?

3. When was Memorial Day officially established as a federal holiday?

4. Why was Memorial Day originally called Decoration Day?

5. Why do you think it is important to honor America's fallen soldiers?

6. What has been America's longest war?

7. Which of America's wars have caused the most deaths?

8. According to President Ronald Reagan, what were the reasons the American soldiers fought for?

9. In the Civil War, which side lost more of the men, as a percentage of the whole society?

10. According to Reagan, what knowledge did American soldiers on the beaches of Normandy have?

RESEARCH OR ANALYSIS:

1. Find an American veteran who has seen combat. Ask him/her for an interview. Review with your classmates what you learned.

2. Look at the various wars the United States has fought. Choose one you know the least about. Research this war and find out basic information. Report your findings to your classmates.

3. Visit (if possible) a Veteran's Museum or the military portion of a local museum with your family or class on Memorial Day.

4. Thank a veteran for his/her service!

CHAPTER SIX
INDEPENDENCE DAY

July 4th

On July 4th, 1776, delegates at the Continental Congress adopted "The Declaration of Independence." This declaration stated that the 13 English colonies were now formally separated from Great Britain and part of a new country, the United States of America. The chief writer of the declaration, Thomas Jefferson, wrote the ideals of the young nation and explained to the world why the states were breaking with the mother country, Great Britain.

Colonial Period

Throughout the 1600s and 1700s, British colonists slowly grew to see themselves as something different from English. At the founding of the first colony in 1607, the most colonists of America were proud of their rights from Great Britain. At the same time, however, those in America enjoyed greater freedoms than the people in all of Europe. In America, for example, many colonists enjoyed the right to vote, to choose their own legislature, and had great economic freedoms.

From 1754-1763, some colonists fought alongside the British in the French and Indian War. In this worldwide conflict, France and England fought over control of North America. In America, a young George Washington distinguished himself as a capable and valiant officer. Washington successfully led a British retreat, after the British General Braddock was killed at the Battle of Monongahela. The British won the war and became the dominant power of North America.

The French and Indian War was a spark to America's independence. During the war, many English colonists realized they were different than the British soldiers. Often, the British officers looked down upon the colonists and did not respect their customs and fighting. After the war, King George III and Parliament faced a huge war debt. To pay off the debt, the English chose to levy taxes on the colonists. As the colonists were not used to being taxed without voting on it, they protested. This eventually led to the separation of the two nations.

The Declaration of Independence

In the Declaration of Independence, Jefferson is inspired from John Locke in writing the ideals of the new nation, "We hold these truths to be self evident: That all men are created equal." The notion that all men are created equal involves a number of ideas. The first is that there is one Creator of all men. Jefferson and the Founding Fathers believed in one God who created all things. The second idea in this statement is that the Creator gave all humans political equality. Paraphrasing John Locke, Jefferson wrote that one Englishman should not have more political rights than another. An important part of equal rights was the right of all men to own private property.

At the time of the Declaration, women could not vote and there were slaves in America. However, Jefferson's writing on political equality was his vision of an ideal. It is important for a people to have an ideal to strive for. Eventually, the U.S.A. would rid itself of slavery, black Americans would enjoy equal political rights, and women would gain the right to vote.

Does political equality mean economic equality? Some people have falsely argued this. Having the same political rights does not mean that a people will be equal in every way. Jefferson did not write that all people will have the same amount of money, for example. This would require the end of freedom, as some people would have their property taken from them by force.

★★★★ CHAPTER SIX | INDEPENDENCE DAY ★★★★

Jefferson continues to borrow from John Locke in writing in the Declaration "that they are endowed by their Creator with certain unalienable rights; that among these are life, liberty, and the pursuit of happiness." These are commonly referred to as the "natural rights." They are natural because man has them through birth. No government gives man these rights. They are his naturally, from God. The right to life means that nobody is allowed to take a human life. Murder is against the law. Liberty means the right to political freedoms, such as the right of free speech, free press, and the right of religious freedom. The pursuit of freedom had commonly been understood to mean the right to own private property, but it also seems to imply more than this. In most places of the world in the 1700s, people did not have the means or rights to acquire and retain property. Property was the right held only by the ruler, or by the ruling class. In the new country of the U.S.A., the American Founding Fathers firmly believed in every man's right to own land. This right allowed a person independence from government, and the ability to establish a family and enjoy the fruits of one's labor.

On July 4th, Americans celebrate Independence Day by spending time with family, watching fireworks, listening to speeches given by military and political leaders, and taking time off from life's work. July 4th may be called America's first federal holiday, because on this day our country established itself as an independent country. On July 4th, take the time to read out loud the Declaration of Independence, and reflect on all of the work America's Founding Fathers put into establishing our country, as well as all of the sacrifices Americans have made for their country over more than two centuries.

QUESTIONS:

1. When was the Declaration of Independence adopted?

2. What did the Declaration of Independence state about the 13 English colonies?

3. Who distinguished himself as a brave soldier during the French and Indian War?

4. Why did the colonists protest the taxes of the English King and Parliament?

5. Where did Thomas Jefferson get his ideas from in writing the Declaration of Independence?

6. What is the difference between political equality and economic equality?

7. What did Jefferson write about the belief in God?

8. Was owning private property normal or unique in the 1700s?

9. Why can July 4th be called America's first federal holiday?

10. How did you celebrate the last July 4th?

RESEARCH OR ANALYSIS:

Students can create a very simple 5 Question quiz on the American Revolution. Then, students ask as many people these questions, keeping track of the score of each person. After asking at least 10 people, students report to the teacher how much, or how little, these 10 people know. The idea behind this is to find out how much Americans know and don't know about the beginning of their country, and to show students the level of knowledge or ignorance of their fellow Americans.

★★★★ CHAPTER SEVEN ★★★★
LABOR DAY

The First Monday in September

Labor Day is celebrated on the first Monday of September. It is a holiday in honor of the workers of the United States of America. Labor Day is typically a celebration of the average city-worker, and was the culmination of a growing labor movement in American cities. It marked the end of a chiefly agrarian society in America and the beginning of a modern one. In 1894, President Grover Cleveland signed the Labor Day legislation into law.

Life on the Farm

It is challenging to remember life in the United States before the era of industrialization. At the time of the American Revolution, 95% of Americans grew up and worked on farms. By the Civil War it was around 60%. By 1900 it was around 40%. Life on a farm is often glamorized, with romantic visions of beautiful sunsets, sweet-smelling grass and corn, and quiet and peace.

In reality, the workday for the typical farmhand in pre-industrial America was tough. Starting at the age of 8 or younger in some circumstances, kids awoke before dawn to feed the animals, clean the stalls, and continued to work throughout the day, as long as the sun was up. A boy did all the work a man would do, from driving tractors to repairing anything that would break. And, his workday was over 12 hours a day. Girls shadowed their mothers, also working over 12 hours a day on household chores like making clothes, food, mending, and taking care of all medicinal needs of the family. Work on the farm was grueling, and at times dangerous. Working with machines and wild animals brought the risk of physical harm to adults and children.

Industrial America

When American society changed from an agrarian society to an industrial one, families faced great challenges, both socially and economically. Before, the family who owned a farm all worked together. In a city, family members worked in different locations. Where most family farms were independently owned in the 1700s and 1800s, workers in cities didn't own the businesses they worked in. And, because America was such a huge attraction to foreigners, city life offered a constantly changing society.

In 1800s America, life for a factory worker was also challenging. Workers had few or no rights, factories could be physically dangerous, and business owners had incredible freedoms how they could treat workers. Workers could be killed by working in dangerous factories, or they could lose limbs and then be fired from their jobs. Still, the American worker did much better than other workers of the world. If this weren't so, the U.S.A. wouldn't have been the destination of so many millions of immigrants.

From 1865-1890, per capita income of Americans doubled! It is during this time that many of America's immigrants passed through Ellis Island in New York. The opportunity of America overrode the hardships of life when it came to where people wanted to live.

Because of the harsh work conditions, American labor leaders sought to gather workers into unions to bargain for worker rights. Initially, there was great opposition to worker rights both by the government and by business owners. In the U.S.A., part of the labor movement wanted a complete takeover of individual business and property rights. Eugene Debs, leader of the American Railways Union, became a Socialist after he led the Pullman Strike in 1894. Socialists wanted workers to take over factories and run them, ideally sharing in all costs and profits. Some socialists were in favor of working for national socialism and others for international socialism.

CHAPTER SEVEN | LABOR DAY

National and International Socialism

In Germany and Italy in the 1920s and 1930's, Adolf Hitler and Benito Mussolini led national socialist parties. In the Soviet Union, Vladimir Lenin and Josef Stalin led an international socialist party, called the Communist Party. Communists favored a worldwide worker's violent revolution. In these socialist systems of Germany, Italy, and the Soviet Union, individuals lost nearly all rights, including the rights of private property. Leaders of these countries were responsible for the murder of tens of millions of people. Americans did not want the same to happen to their country because of a promise of a worker's paradise.

The American Labor Movement

In the United States, some labor leaders focused on making the lives of workers better by pushing for an 8 hour workday, safer work conditions, and demanding fair treatment of all workers in every situation. These leaders chose not to take political power, but to work for social and economic change within the system. These leaders were not interested in a socialist rebellion or to deny individuals their rights. Samuel Gompers was one such union leader. From 1886 – 1894, he was President of the American Federation of Labor. Gompers pushed for American workers to enjoy rights within the capitalist system, and fought other union leaders who wanted to transform the U.S. into a socialist system. By promoting worker rights within a capitalistic society, he helped establish a distinctly American form of unionism.

In 1894, railway workers in the American Railway Union led by Eugene Debs demanded better work conditions and went on strike against the Pullman Company. The U.S. government and other unions crushed it with violence. 30 workers were killed.

President Cleveland and the U.S. Congress initially opposed the strike, but later realized that many of the workers' demands were reasonable. The Pullman Company was forced to change in favor of the workers. In 1894, the U.S. government passed a law declaring the first Monday of September a national holiday to honor workers.

Labor Day Belittled

Because in 1967, Congress passed a law moving this holiday to the closest Monday, its original meaning has been destroyed. Today, this holiday is mainly celebrated as a seasonal event, with families marking it as the end of summer and beginning of fall.

QUESTIONS:

1. About when did most Americans work in industry?

2. At about which age did American kids begin working on the family farm and how many hours a day did they work?

3. Name two differences from working in cities to working on farms.

4. In the early 1900s, what might happen to a factory worker if he lost his arm due to an accident at work?

5. Why did immigrants come to the U.S.A. in large numbers in the last half of the 19th century?

6. What happened in Germany, Italy, and the Soviet Union in the 1920s and 1930s?

7. What did Samuel Gompers want for workers in America?

8. How did Gomper's goals differ from the Socialists' goals in Germany, Italy, and the Soviet Union?

9. What happened in the Pullman Strike of the late 1890s?

10. What year did the first Labor Day in the U.S.A. occur?

RESEARCH OR ANALYSIS:

Direct your children to interview three people (one of them needs to own his own business) and ask five questions about the work he or she does. After the three interviews, have your children decide what sounds good about each of the three jobs/professions and what sounds unpleasant. Have a short discussion about what type of work your child could imagine doing.

Here are sample questions for the interview:

a. Can you describe a typical day at work?

b. What is the pay range for your field?

c. What are the highs and lows of your job?

d. What education is required for your job?

e. If you could give me one piece of advice regarding my future work, what would it be?

CHAPTER EIGHT
COLUMBUS DAY

Second Monday in October

Christopher Columbus (1451-1506) was an explorer, cartographer (map maker), and adventurer from the Republic of Genoa (today it is part of northern Italy). In 1492, he led an expedition from Spain and discovered the islands of the West Indies in the Caribbean Sea of the "New World." He died believing he had found a westerly route to Asia, but in reality he had opened up the continents of North America and South America for European discovery and colonization. Fifty years ago, Americans viewed Columbus as a hero, and schoolchildren across the country had the day off from school. Today, Columbus is honored by students in only a few states, and in many parts of our country he is viewed with great dislike. Columbus Day is celebrated in some places of the United States on the second Monday of October, sometimes falling on the day he discovered America, October 12th, 1492.

A Man of the Renaissance

In the 1400s, Western Europeans rapidly modernized, experienced a social mobility never before imaginable, developed high forms of art, and used technology in new ways. The Renaissance that had started in Italian city-states had spread north, and throughout Europe there was a sense that the world was waiting to be explored, discovered, conquered and civilized by those brave and eager enough to do so. The Renaissance was a time where European artists and intellectuals rediscovered the beauty of ancient Greece and Rome. City-states in Italy grew wealthy from trade with the East through the Mediterranean Sea, and countries in Western Europe wanted to be able to travel directly to the East by the ocean, without having to go across the Mediterranean Sea and deal with middle men. In 1492, the Spanish finally succeeded in liberating Spain from the African Muslims who had controlled them for over 700 years. After this 700-year war, Spain was filled with unbound confidence and believed it was a chosen country to explore, Christianize, and conquer the world.

Ocean travel is challenging, but the Renaissance mindset, Spanish confidence, new technology, and vision of Christopher Columbus made such a huge journey possible. His dream as an adult was to sale west from Europe and go straight to Asia, where he could open up new trade routes with China. Nobody, of course, knew that in-between Asia and Europe were the Americas. Nearly all sailors knew that the Earth was round, however, no sailor knew how far the journey from Europe to the next continent would be, and there was fear of starving if Asia was not reached. The Asian invention of the astrolabe, an instrument that made travelling at night and away from shore possible, helped sailors like Columbus have greater confidence to sail far away.

Columbus Sails West

King Ferdinand and Queen Isabella of Spain, fresh from their victory over the Muslims in 1492, agreed to allow Columbus to use Spanish ships and men pursue his quest. Columbus set out in three ships: the Nina, the Pinta, and the Santa Maria. His goals were to find a new trade route to Asia, to find gold and bring it back to Spain, to claim new land for Spain, and to spread Catholic Christianity throughout the world. After approximately 30 days, Columbus found new land, however, it was not Asia, it was an island in the Bahamas, which he named "San Salvador," the Savior. Columbus believed he had found India and called the natives "Indians."

Columbus made four different journeys to the Americas, established Spanish forts, was completely unsuccessful in finding any gold, and was arrested by the Spanish for being an incompetent and tyrannical governor of the new lands. Columbus' men were so intent on finding gold that they mistreated many of the Indians. There are historical accounts of torture and murder by some of Columbus' men, and Columbus was either unable, or unwilling to stop them. The group of Indians Columbus first encountered, the Tainos, were extinct 50 years later. Most Indians who came into contact with the Spanish and other Europeans died from diseases, such as small pox. The natives did not have these diseases, and had no immunity built

★★★★ CHAPTER EIGHT | COLUMBUS DAY ★★★★

up against them. The Spanish King and Queen eventually arrested Columbus, had him brought him back in chains, tried him for incompetence and for the cruel treatment some of his men perpetrated against the Indians, and jailed him. In six weeks, the King released him.

Columbus Legacy

Columbus' legacy in the new world is mixed. He discovered America and opened up new lands for the rest of the world. Before Columbus, Indians in the Americas worshipped many gods, many practiced torture and polygamy, and some practiced cannibalism as a way of life. Europeans who came and eventually settled the Americas brought monotheism, ended polygamy, and brought literacy to the Indians. Eventually, the United States of America was founded, as were all other modern nations of North and South America.

Columbus has been the focus of those who argue that the European conquest of the Americas was an immoral act against the Indians. European disease, such as small pox, is believed to have killed up to 90% of the Indian population. And, the superior strength of Europeans meant that it was easier to destroy the Indian culture. Before the 1960s, American students and historians focused on the positive elements of Columbus' discovery of America, and all America celebrated him. In 1971, Columbus Day became a federal holiday. After this, however, certain states began to eliminate the celebration of Columbus. In California, for example, students do not celebrate Columbus Day, and a public school teacher may hear his colleagues berate Christopher Columbus. In New York, however, Columbus is heralded as a hero, and New York City has a huge Columbus Day Parade that involves over 35,000 people every year.

Was Columbus a hero or not? That is a great question to ponder on Columbus Day, which is a federal holiday in the United States of America on October 14th (but is celebrated on the second Monday of October.) In many states where Columbus Day is not celebrated, students have stopped learning about him altogether. Unfortunately, it appears most American students do not even know anything about Christopher Columbus.

QUESTIONS:

1. Who was Columbus and what did he do?

2. Why is Columbus honored in some states and not in others?

3. What ended in Spain in 1492? What role did this play in Columbus' discovery?

4. Why do we say Columbus discovered America when there were already people living there?

5. Was Columbus considered a success by the king and queen of Spain?

6. Which practices of some of the Native Americans did the Spanish stop? What do you think of the Spanish telling the Americans that they couldn't continue these practices?

7. What did nearly all Americans think of Columbus before the 1960s?

8. When did Columbus Day become a federal holiday?

9. What killed most Indians that came into contact with Europeans?

10. Where is at least one place where Columbus Day is still celebrated?

RESEARCH OR ANALYSIS:

Have a discussion or write a short essay: Was Columbus a hero or not?

★★★★ CHAPTER EIGHT | COLUMBUS DAY ★★★★

ACTIVITES:

IN 1492

In fourteen hundred ninety-two
Columbus sailed the ocean blue.
He had three ships and left from Spain;
He sailed through sunshine, wind and rain.
He sailed by night; he sailed by day;
He used the stars to find his way.
A compass also helped him know
How to find the way to go.
Ninety sailors were on board;
Some men worked while others snored.
Then the workers went to sleep;
And others watched the ocean deep.
Day after day they looked for land;
They dreamed of trees and rocks and sand.
October 12 their dream came true,
You never saw a happier crew!
"Indians! Indians!" Columbus cried;
His heart was filled with joyful pride.
But "India" the land was not;
It was the Bahamas, and it was hot.
The Arakawa natives were very nice;
They gave the sailors food and spice.
Columbus sailed on to find some gold
To bring back home, as he'd been told.
He made the trip again and again,
Trading gold to bring to Spain.
The first American? No, not quite.
But Columbus was brave, and he was bright.

COLUMBUS DAY SONG

(sung to the tune of "The Farmer in the Dell")

In 1492,

In 1492,

Columbus sailed across the sea,

In 1492.

33 days he sailed,

33 days he sailed,

Columbus sailed across the sea,

33 days he sailed.

He came to a new land,

He came to a new land,

Columbus sailed across the sea,

And came to a new land.

Exploring he did go,

Exploring he did go,

Columbus sailed across the sea,

Exploring he did go.

He sailed back home to Spain,

He sailed back home to Spain,

Columbus sailed across the sea,

Then sailed back home to Spain.

THE THREE SHIPS

The Nina, the Pinta, the Santa Maria.

Three little ships from Spain,

Sailed over the seas, under skies so blue,

Sailed on through the wind and rain.

So brave was the captain,

So gallant his rew,

Their faith remained steadfast,

Till their goal came in view.

The Nina, the Pinta, the Santa Maria,

Three little ships from Spain,

Inspired the later pioneers

Who settled on hill and plain,

So great was their labor,

Their courage so true,

That our mighty nation

From their striving grew!

Lillian W. Allard

CHAPTER NINE
VETERAN'S DAY

November 11th

World War I – known at the time as "The Great War" - officially ended when the Treaty of Versailles was signed on June 28, 1919, in the Palace of Versailles outside the town of Versailles, France. However, fighting ceased seven months earlier when an armistice, or temporary cessation of hostilities, between the Allied nations and Germany went into effect on the eleventh hour of the eleventh day of the eleventh month. For that reason, November 11, 1918, is generally regarded as the end of "the war to end all wars."

On June 4, 1918, The United States Congress officially recognized the end of World War I with these words:

"Whereas the 11th of November 1918, marked the cessation of the most destructive, sanguinary, and far reaching war in human annals and the resumption by the people of the United States of peaceful relations with other nations, which we hope may never again be severed, and

Whereas it is fitting that the recurring anniversary of this date should be commemorated with thanksgiving and prayer and exercises designed to perpetuate peace through good will and mutual understanding between nations; and

Whereas the legislatures of twenty-seven of our States have already declared November 11 to be a legal holiday: Therefore be it Resolved by the Senate (the House of Representatives concurring), that the President of the United States is requested to issue a proclamation calling upon the officials to display the flag of the United States on all Government buildings on November 11 and inviting the people of the United States to observe the day in schools and churches, or other suitable places, with appropriate ceremonies of friendly relations with all other peoples."

In 1938, Congress declared that November 11th be set aside for prayer and thanksgiving for the end of World War I. However, after World War II and the Korean War, the U.S. Congress decided to change this day to Veterans Day, thus honoring veterans of all wars.

Veteran's Day Proclamation

On October 8th, President Dwight D. Eisenhower issued the first Veteran's Day Proclamation, which stated: "In order to insure proper and widespread observance of this anniversary, all veterans, all veterans' organizations, and the entire citizenry will wish to join hands in the common purpose. Toward this end, I am designating the Administrator of Veterans' Affairs as Chairman of a Veterans Day National Committee, which shall include such other persons as the Chairman may select, and which will coordinate at the national level necessary planning for the observance. I am also requesting the heads of all departments and agencies of the Executive branch of the Government to assist the National Committee in every way possible."

In 1968, by an act of Congress, Veteran's Day and three other holidays were moved to Mondays, so Americans could celebrate these days with a three day weekend. Many complained that this took away from the original purpose of the holidays. In 1975, President Ford signed into law to observe Veteran's Day on November 11, when it is celebrated today.

★★★ CHAPTER NINE | VETERAN'S DAY ★★★

A poem written by Canadian soldier John McCrae during World War I is often remembered by those studying World War I. Flanders is a town in the country of Belgium. Major John McCrae was a military doctor and artillery commander, and it is believed he wrote this poem after witnessing a friend killed in war and burying him.

In Flanders Fields

by John McCrae, May 1915:

In Flanders fields the poppies blow

Between the crosses, row on row,

That mark our place; and in the sky

The larks, still bravely singing, fly

Scarce heard amid the guns below.

We are the Dead. Short days ago

We lived, felt dawn, saw sunset glow,

Loved and were loved, and now we lie

In Flanders fields.

Take up our quarrel with the foe:

To you from failing hands we throw

The torch; be yours to hold it high.

If ye break faith with us who die

We shall not sleep, though poppies grow

In Flanders fields.

QUESTIONS:

1. Read out loud the poem, twice.

2. What date is Veteran's Day?

3. Why was this particular date chosen for Veteran's Day?

4. What treaty ended World War I?

5. What were the intentions of the U.S. Congress as to how November 11th would be commemorated?

6. When was Armistice Day changed to Veteran's Day? Why?

7. Why did President Ford sign into law to commemorate Veteran's Day on November 11th?

8. What did John McCrae write in May 1915?

9. What does "The Dead" urge the living to do in the poem by John McCrae?

10. Based on the poem, was John McCrae urging others to continue fighting or stop fighting?

RESEARCH OR ANALYSIS:

1. In your own words, write what Major John McCrae's poem means.

2. What does Major John think about the war? What words from the poem let you know this?

3. Is this poem an anti-war poem, or is it an inspiring poem for soldiers to continue fighting?

4. What words from the poem let you know this?

5. Interview a war veteran and ask him/her about his experiences in the war.

CHAPTER TEN
THANKSGIVING DAY

The Fourth Thursday in November

The Pilgrims in Europe

In the early 1600s, a group of people called Pilgrims left England to find a new home where they could practice their religion freely. In England, everyone who was not a member of the Church of England (or, Anglicans) was persecuted. The Pilgrims were not Anglicans. They went to Holland where there was religious freedom.

In Holland, the Pilgrims could practice their religion freely, however, they were not happy. Their children were learning to speak Dutch, practice Dutch customs, and were losing their English culture. Also, in England, the Pilgrims had been farmers, but in Holland, they lived in the cities. Because of these reasons, the Pilgrims decided to leave Holland.

After returning to England for a short time, the Pilgrims left for America in 1620. After sailing 65 days, they landed their ship, The Mayflower, in the New World. The Pilgrims were supposed to join the settlers of Jamestown in Virginia, but a storm had blown them off course. Before stepping ashore, they wrote The Mayflower Compact, a short document declaring every person's intention to glorify God, follow the laws, and to honor the King of England. It was the first self-written governing document in the New World. 102 English citizens set foot in America and founded Plymouth, in present-day Massachusetts. The Pilgrims stayed on their ship until homes could be built out of the wood from the forest.

Pilgrims in America

The first year was incredibly harsh for the Pilgrims. Of the 102, 45 people died during a few months. Of the eighteen women, only four survived that first year. The Pilgrims were unaccustomed to the harsh winters of the Northeast, and did not know which crops grew best.

One day in Spring, an Indian walked up to the Pilgrims, and to their surprise, spoke English and befriended the Europeans. Samoset had lived among English speakers for a time as a slave, and when he retained his freedom, he went back to his people in the Northeast of America. Samoset and his friend Squanto taught the Pilgrims what crops to grow and how to use fish as a fertilizer. He also acted as a peaceful contact between Chief Massosoit and the Pilgrims.

In the fall, the Pilgrims, a very religious people, decided to set aside a time to honor God and give him thanks for all of their blessings. It is amazing to think of the faith, courage, and humility of these people. In a year, half of them had died in a cold and cruel climate. They were far from their friends and comforts. And still, they wanted to have a number of days set aside to give God thanks for their blessings. They invited their neighbors, the Indians, to show them thanks for their help, and to include them in their feast.

The first Thanksgiving in America lasted for three days, involved all of the Pilgrims (approximately 50), and 90 Indian men. It is believed the Indian women did not attend because the Indians did not trust the Englishmen. During these three days, Indians played competitive games, and the English and Indians shared the best foods together.

CHAPTER TEN | THANKSGIVING DAY

A few years later, in 1623, Massachusetts governor William Bradford, wrote America's first Thanksgiving Proclamation. He set aside a specific day and time for the citizens to honor God for his blessings. Beginning with President George Washington, U.S. Presidents have issued a Thanksgiving Proclamation, as well. In 1863, in the middle of the American Civil War, where over 600,000 Americans were killed, President Abraham Lincoln declared that the last Thursday in November be set aside as… "a day of Thanksgiving and Praise to our beneficent Father who dwelleth in the Heavens." Lincoln's proclamation made Thanksgiving Day a federal holiday.

America's First Thanksgiving Proclamation by Governor Bradford

Inasmuch as the great Father has given us this year an abundant harvest of Indian corn, wheat, peas, beans, squashes, and garden vegetables, and has made the forests to abound with game and the sea with fish and clams, and inasmuch as he has protected us from the ravages of the savages, has spared us from pestilence and disease, has granted us freedom to worship God according to the dictates of our own conscience.

Now I, your magistrate, do proclaim that all ye Pilgrims, with your wives and ye little ones, do gather at ye meeting house, on ye hill, between the hours of 9 and 12 in the day time, on Thursday, November 29th, of the year of our Lord one thousand six hundred and twenty-three and the third year since ye Pilgrims landed on ye Pilgrim Rock, there to listen to ye pastor and render thanksgiving to ye Almighty God for all His blessings.

William Bradford | Ye Governor of Ye Colony | 1623

Thanksgiving Proclamation of President George Washington

WHEREAS, It is the duty of all nations to acknowledge the providence of Almighty God, to obey His will, to be grateful for His benefits, and humbly to implore His protection and favor;

WHEREAS, Both the houses of Congress have, by their joint committee, requested me "to recommend to the people of the United States a day of public thanksgiving and prayer, to be observed by acknowledging with grateful hearts the many and signal favors of Almighty God, especially by affording them an opportunity peaceably to establish a form of government for their safety and happiness:"

Now, therefore, I do recommend and assign Thursday, the 26th day of November next, to be devoted by the people of these States to the service of that great and glorious Being who is the beneficent author of all the good that was, that is, or that will be; that we may then all unite in rendering unto Him our sincere and humble thanks for His kind care and protection of the people of this country previous to their becoming a nation; for the signal and manifold mercies and the favorable interpositions of His providence in the course and conclusion of the late war; for the great degree of tranquility, union, and plenty which we have since enjoyed; for the peaceable and rational manner in which we have been able to establish constitutions of government for our safety and happiness, and particularly the national one now lately instituted for the civil and religious liberty with which we are blessed, and the means we have of acquiring and diffusing useful knowledge; and, in general, for all the great and various favors which He has been pleased to confer upon us.

And also that we may then unite in most humbly offering our prayers and supplications to the great Lord and Ruler of Nations and beseech Him to pardon our national and other transgressions; to enable us all, whether in public or private stations, to perform our several and relative duties properly and punctually; to render our National Government a blessing to all the people by constantly being a Government of wise, just, and constitutional laws, discreetly and faithfully executed and obeyed; to protect and guide all sovereigns and nations (especially such as have show kindness to us), and to bless them with good governments, peace, and concord; to promote the knowledge and practice of true religion and virtue, and the increase of science among them and us; and, generally to grant unto all mankind such a degree of temporal prosperity as He alone knows to be best.

--George Washington - October 3, 1789

President Abraham Lincoln's Thanksgiving Day Proclamation That Established the National Holiday

Washington, D.C. | October 3, 1863

By the President of the United States of America.

A Proclamation.

The year that is drawing towards its close, has been filled with the blessings of fruitful fields and healthful skies. To these bounties, which are so constantly enjoyed that we are prone to forget the source from which they come, others have been added, which are of so extraordinary a nature, that they cannot fail to penetrate and soften even the heart which is habitually insensible to the ever watchful providence of Almighty God. In the midst of a civil war of unequaled magnitude and severity, which has sometimes seemed to foreign States to invite and to provoke their aggression, peace has been preserved with all nations, order has been maintained, the laws have been respected and obeyed, and harmony has prevailed everywhere except in the theatre of military conflict; while that theatre has been greatly contracted by the advancing armies and navies of the Union. Needful diversions of wealth and of strength from the fields of peaceful industry to the national defence, have not arrested the plough, the shuttle or the ship; the axe has enlarged the borders of our settlements, and the mines, as well of iron and coal as of the

★★★ CHAPTER TEN | THANKSGIVING DAY ★★★

precious metals, have yielded even more abundantly than heretofore. Population has steadily increased, notwithstanding the waste that has been made in the camp, the siege and the battle-field; and the country, rejoicing in the consciousness of augmented strength and vigor, is permitted to expect continuance of years with large increase of freedom.

No human counsel hath devised nor hath any mortal hand worked out these great things. They are the gracious gifts of the Most High God, who, while dealing with us in anger for our sins, hath nevertheless remembered mercy. It has seemed to me fit and proper that they should be solemnly, reverently and gratefully acknowledged as with one heart and one voice by the whole American People.

I do therefore invite my fellow citizens in every part of the United States, and also those who are at sea and those who are sojourning in foreign lands, to set apart and observe the last Thursday of November next, as a day of Thanksgiving and Praise to our beneficent Father who dwelleth in the Heavens. And I recommend to them that while offering up the ascriptions justly due to Him for such singular deliverances and blessings, they do also, with humble penitence for our national perverseness and disobedience, commend to His tender care all those who have become widows, orphans, mourners or sufferers in the lamentable civil strife in which we are unavoidably engaged, and fervently implore the interposition of the Almighty Hand to heal the wounds of the nation and to restore it as soon as may be consistent with the Divine purposes to the full enjoyment of peace, harmony, tranquillity and Union.

In testimony whereof, I have hereunto set my hand and caused the Seal of the United States to be affixed.

Done at the City of Washington, this Third day of October, in the year of our Lord one thousand eight hundred and sixty-three, and of the Independence of the Unites States the Eighty-eighth.

By the President: Abraham Lincoln, 1863

QUESTIONS:

1. Who were the Pilgrims who set sail for North America in 1620 and why did they leave England?

2. What was the significance of the Mayflower Compact?

3. What happened during the Pilgrims' first year in America?

4. Who helped the Pilgrims survive after the harsh winter?

5. Why did the Pilgrims hold a celebration of Thanksgiving after having lost nearly half of the people who originally came to America?

6. In 1623, Governor Bradford wrote America's first Thanksgiving Proclamation. Who did he intend the Pilgrims to give thanks to?

7. In President Washington's Thanksgiving Proclamation, for what is he most thankful to God for?

8. Paraphrase the first sentence of the third paragraph of Washington's Proclamation.

9. In Abraham Lincoln's Thanksgiving Day Proclamation of 1863, who did Lincoln say the U.S. should give thanks to?

10. Write down five things that you are thankful for.

RESEARCH OR ANALYSIS:

1. Interview five people older than you. Ask them what the history and meaning of Thanksgiving are. Share with your classmates how many people knew the history and meaning of Thanksgiving.

2. How can Americans best keep alive the history and meaning of Thanksgiving?

★★★★ CHAPTER ELEVEN ★★★★
CHRISTMAS DAY

December 25th

In the United States of America, Christmas was established as a federal holiday on June 26, 1870. It is a celebration of the birth of Jesus Christ, the man Christians believe is the son of God and the savior of the world. Christmas has its roots in ancient times and is celebrated around the world.

The Three Kings

For the first few hundred years after Jesus Christ, his birthday was not celebrated. Instead, Epiphany, when the three kings from separate places of the world visited Christ, was the focus of Christians. The visit of the Magi symbolized that salvation was open to the whole world, not just one select nation. Later, early Church Fathers began to write that the birth of Jesus Christ should be celebrated. December 25, 336, marks the first day Christians in the Roman Empire officially celebrated the first Christmas on Earth.

The Date of Christmas

The date of Christmas and some American traditions have pagan roots. In the Roman Empire, December 25th was the day of "natalis solis invict" (the Roman birth of the sun), and the birthday of Mithras, the Iranian "Sun of Righteousness." Saturnalia, a Roman festival that honored the sun, lasted from December 17th to December 23rd. The winter solstice, the darkest day of the year, also falls a few days before December 25th and had been celebrated by pagans. Early Christian Church leaders believed that days that had been set aside to honor pagan gods could be changed to honor Christianity. It was thought that people would more easily accept Christianity and move away from paganism by replacing pagan celebrations with Christian ones.

The festival of Saturnalia honored the Roman god Saturn. Romans had a public banquet, gifts were exchanged, there was much partying, and servants were served by their masters. Singers performed in streets, and baked cookies shaped like men. While some Christians dislike any association with pagan traditions, one early Christian writer commented, "We hold this day holy, not like the pagans because of the birth of the sun, but because of Him who made it."

Christmas Celebrations Outlawed

In Great Britain, Christmas was celebrated until the Puritans, led by Oliver Cromwell, outlawed Christmas in 1645. Puritans believed that celebrating the birth of Christ was a sign of decadence and a disgrace to Christianity. In the English Colonies, the English Separatists also believed in worshipping Jesus without ceremonies and made celebrating Christmas a crime.

Christmas in America

In the 1800s, Americans' views on Christmas changed a great deal. One New York author, Washington Irving, wrote stories of how Christmas had been celebrated in England before the Puritans took over, and some of these stories caught on in American practices. German immigrants brought with them the practice of placing evergreen branches and trees in homes during winter. Evergreen branches and trees were a reminder of spring and growth. And, Catholic immigrants brought the tradition started by Saint Francis of keeping small nativity scenes in their homes. By the late 1800s, most Americans celebrated Christmas, and thus, in 1870, the federal government declared it a national holiday.

★★★★ CHAPTER ELEVEN | CHRISTMAS DAY ★★★★

QUESTIONS:

1. What is Christmas a celebration of?

2. What day did early Christians celebrate that was not the birthday of Jesus?

3. What is "natalis solis invict" and on what day did Romans celebrate it?

4. Why did early Christian leaders choose a date that used to be a pagan holiday to celebrate Christmas?

5. What was the festival of Saturnalia?

6. Who outlawed the celebration of Christmas in 1645? Why?

7. What did English Separatists in the colonies think about celebrating Christmas?

8. What did Washington Irving write about Christmas?

9. What did German immigrants to America practice regarding Christmas?

10. Who created the idea of the nativity scene?

RESEARCH OR ANALYSIS:

1. Research how Christmas is celebrated in three other countries. Write this down. Choose one tradition that you find most interesting. Share this with your family.

2. Research the history behind Santa Claus. Who was Saint Nicholaus? When did he live?

ABOUT THE CLASSICAL HISTORIAN

After working in private and public and home school education for over twenty years, John realized the great need in American society to promote independent and critical thinking through research and thoughtful discussion. His wife Zdenka, born and raised in Czechoslovakia, could not find fun and beautiful games that taught their children history. John and Zdenka founded The Classical Historian (www.classicalhistorian.com) to fill these two voids. Their materials are inspired by the best that is offered in the Western tradition of education: openness, analysis, healthy competition in games, respect towards opposing viewpoints, recognition of an absolute truth, and academic honesty. The Classical Historian teaches students what they want to know how they want to learn. John and Zdenka De Gree home school their children in San Clemente, California.

BOOK DESIGN: JASON PEARSON

Jason runs Pearpod, a small boutique agency in San Clemente, California. Pearpod develops projects for non-profits and faith intiatives, including: World Vision, Scripture Union, Saddleback Church, and American Bible Society. Jason has also developed design and marketing for Hollywood faith & family films such as The Passion of the Christ, Narnia, Trade of Innocents and Son of God. Jason and his wife Melinda home school their five kids (including triplets).

DISCOVER MORE GREAT RESOURCES AT CLASSICALHISTORIAN.COM

Made in the USA
Columbia, SC
11 July 2024

38342236R00035